Anonymous

Cuba

Anonymous

Cuba

ISBN/EAN: 9783337728663

Printed in Europe, USA, Canada, Australia, Japan

Cover: Foto ©ninafisch / pixelio.de

More available books at **www.hansebooks.com**

CUBA.

...

GMENTS OF A LETTER

dressed to a Distinguished Party in May, 1869,

WITH NOTES AND APPENDIX.

- • -

ALSO,

REPORT

OF

MARSHAL SERRANO, DUKE de la TORRE,

[PRESENT REGENT OF SPAIN.]

*On the Interrogatories Submitted to him by the Spanish
Government in the matter of Reform in the
regime of the Antilles.*

TRANS   ANISH.

NEW   1869.

CUBA.

FRAGMENTS OF A LETTER ADDRESSED TO A DISTINGUISHED
PARTY, IN MAY, 1869.

❊ ❊ ❊ ❊ ❊ ❊ ❊

I feel that I am unavoidably called upon, in view of the
serious events which occur in Cuba, to give you my testimony. ❊ ❊ ❊ ❊

I wish to call your attention to the following essential
points in relation to Cuba.

1st. That a state of anarchy prevails there beyond
the power of the Spanish Government to control. The
murders committed both in the city of Havana and in
country districts where no war had taken place, the vain
efforts of Gen. Dulce at first to govern and establish a more
legal existence, and his later sanction and praise of the re-
proved acts : the anomalous judiciary ; the transfer of cases
from one to-another so-called court, subject to no written
code of procedure, and coerced by armed Spanish Guards ;—
the exorbitant taxes growing at a rate inconsistent with a
surplus to cover the wants of the population : these evils
either ascertained through skillful agents of this Government
or easily proven by the Spanish organs in Cuba, establish a
state of anarchy which constitutes a distinct trait from the
rude warfare where the war does exist. Such a state pre-
cludes the possibility of guarding the interests, the rights, the
property and the lives of the citizens of the United States :
moreover the condition herein depicted is different from
that exhibited under any circumstances in any christian
state during the second half of the present century.

2d. The proclamation of Gen. Valmaseda beyond the overt sanction of savage warfare adds nothing to what has been silently *practiced* in the Western Department and at Havana where no fighting has been reported nor any insurrectionary movement beyond general restlessness and the gathering and dispersion of Jaguey-Grande.

3d. It would be easy to enter into a detailed account of the incidents which fully settle my convictions regarding the anarchy in Cuba, and I would be ready to do so were it considered necessary. I will simply say now that it is positively known that neither Don Juan Poey, nor Don Julian Zulueta, nor Don Francisco Ibanez, wealthy Europeans, heretofore exercising vast influence in the Spanish party, have power to control the insubordinate volunteers, and hence their discouragement and despair of peace and order being restored are beyond doubt. Is anything more required to prove anarchy than such testimony from the leading men of the Spanish party? (a)

4th. The Spanish dealers, generally speaking, are bankrupt, their business is dependent on the credit of the Spanish Bank which owes its life to the debt of the local government :—trade, beyond the selling of the sugar crops is at stand, and the Spanish clerks are on half pay.

5th. Of the 1,500,000 (b.) inhabitants assigned to Cuba in round numbers, the European Spaniards make with the troops 100,000 of which 35,000 are volunteers disseminated through the island, 13,000 of whom guard the city and forts of Havana and of these, the most desperate govern the remainder, composed of respectable conservative men. The

(a.) As late as the 26th of June, the interference and direct action of the volunteers in the judiciary, the cowardly assassinations committed under the uniform, and the ejection of Gen'l Dulce and others, &c., have confirmed the statements in this letter.

(b.) See appendix No. 1.

45υ,000 (*a.*) slaves counted in the above total would have been emancipated ere this, had the petition of the Cuban representatives manifested at Madrid in 1867 been listened to, and not overruled by the slave-traders and their kind now in power in that island. (*b.*)

6th. The American shipping and the business in produce, hardware, lumber and provisions which at present absorbs a vast amount of American capital and labor, and the claims of American creditors (*c.*) would be suddenly lost if the anarchical condition herein described were to continue a little longer.

(*a.*) According to reliable statistics there are only 370,553 slaves of whom 288,214 are dedicated to agricultural pursuits comprising sugar and coffee estates, farms, cattle pasture grounds, tobacco plantations, etc., throughout the whole island.

(*b.*) After expatiating on the means of emancipating the slaves, the commissioners of the Antilles in the report of 26th April, 1867, signed by Anto. Rodriguez, Ogea, Nicolas Azcarate, Jose Anto. Echevarria Jose de la Cruz Castellanos, Jose Morales Lemus, Jose Miguel Angulo, Count Pozos—Dulces, Manuel de Ortega, Agustin Camejo, Calixto Bernal, Thomas Terry, Geronimo M. Usera, Jose Julian Acosta and Ruiz Belvis express themselves in the following terms:

"It is to be hoped therefore, that the plan will cause no derangement, especially if the "masters convinced, as they ought to be, that the solution of the problem is unavoidable, "will contribute with good will and patriotism to its success. On it depends the sensible "advantage of the present generation and the quiet and happiness of those to come. Wo to "those who shall oppose it!"

(c) That the importance of American commerce may be properly appreciated, we give the following relative proportion of the movement of trade from the statistics of Fernandez Corredor.

United States of America	35.94	per Cent.
England	22.52	"
Spain	19.48	"
France	8.33	"
Germany, Holland and Belgium	7.02	"
Spanish America	4.49	"
Denmark, Sweden, Italy and Norway	1.84	"
Austria, Russia and Portugal	0.15	"
China, Rio Congo and San Domingo	0.04	"
	99.81	
Mercantile Depot	0.19	
	100.00	

If the industry of Cuba, heretofore burdened beyond bounds, were to be subjected to the rising taxation now in progress, general bankruptcy would ensue and foreign commerce would be also ruined.

Such would be the obvious consequence of the forced rule the Spaniards are bent on imposing.

7th. Owing to the lack of a saving municipal structure, and to the irregular and conflicting policy of the metropolitan government, the United States cannot reasonably expect to obtain in Cuba security for Americans by waiting the action of time. If the present strife continue, by the time Spain ceases to send troops, the savage struggle will have caused irreparable ruin. And could Spain maintain a forcible hold, Cuba would be unable to sustain a healthy trade and credit, and to pay the claims of foreign commerce.

We may ere long hear of business derangement in Maine, where the Cuban lumber trade is important, from the number who live by it, rather than from its intrinsic value. Great capitalists may have cautiously placed their own in security, anticipating wisely the present troubles, but the bulk of the commercial interest will suddenly suffer the consequence of past misrule and actual revolution.

8th. When we think that there were 24,000 regular troops at the commencement of the revolution, that 18,000 have arrived since, and that every one of them is employed in the distant pursuit of patriots, leaving the capital and its fortifications in the hands of volunteers, all efforts to diminish the importance of the movement are idle. Its great power is also evinced in the stringent measures adopted by the Spanish authorities. The suppression of the free press, the peculiar judiciary under inspection of the Governor and Police ; the closing of small ports for the exportation of produce, the prohibition of meetings of the smallest number of persons ; the sanctioned arrest of native citizens by privates of the Volunteer Corps ; the separation of natives from those regiments ; the prohibition to bear arms and the seizure of the same from peaceful native citizens ; the unheard-of harshness in the treatment and seclusion of persons under arrest— the sequestration of property, the public murders and executions, etc.

9th. Another significant trait of the present rule at Havana is the announcement through the press of a determination to hold the power now in their hands, whatever government be established in Spain, and to reject particularly the republican form, and any decree favorable to the emancipation of the slaves.

10th. The present accidental ruling power of Cuba has no legitimate origin ; it does not conform to the requirements of civilized nations : it is unable to protect life and property:— those whose authority is paramount there, are knowingly inimical to the government of Washington, and the privileges guaranteed by the treaty of 1795 of progressive liberality in trade; and judgment of American citizens by common law cannot be obtained under such a rule.

11th. Who rules in Cuba ?

Not the King or Queen, because the nation has proclaimed the soverignty of the people :—not the Madrid Provisional Government because we read daily enactments of Gen. Dulce altering the fundamental laws and the most sacred rights.

Neither is Gen. Dulce able to govern according to his own will for his orders are executed only so long as they conform to the sanguinary wishes of the volunteers ;—and certainly the legitimate *majority* of the population have no participation in this iron rule, nor in the imposition of taxes, nor in the recent suppression of schools and other establishments of public interest—all of which measures are the work of official awed and controled.

12th. Having mentioned the present so called Spanish rule in Cuba, I beg leave to submit the following rapid sketch intended to point out where we may find the legitimate government of Cuba sustained by *the assembled vote of its inhabitants of all classes.*

Down to 32 years ago Cuba had always followed the fate of Spain, submitting to absolute power or entering into the exercise of popular franchises accordingly as the one or the other system prevailed in the Peninsula.

Under the Bourbons an assembly of planters and merchants freely elected, and hereditary municipalities, independent of the crown, were to a certain extent a proper substitute for Provincial assemblies. (*a*)

In 1812, Cuba enjoyed in common with Spain, a democratic government and sent deputies to the court.

In 1814, on the return of Ferdinand, both Spain and Cuba were again subjected to absolute rule.

In 1820, constitutional government was restored in both the metropolis and the Colony.

In 1823, at the bidding of Louis the 18th, the absolute power of Ferdinand the 7th was restored to both, and the three deputies of Cuba arrived in this City of New York and became known as men of high moral standing : Thomas Gener, Felix Varela, and Leonardo Santos Suarez.

In 1834, the Estatuto Real placed Cuba again in the enjoyment of the same rights with Spain, and she sent deputies once more.

At last in one of the many political changes Spain has undergone, the representatives of all the provinces were con-

(*a*) For the election to the ancient institution called Consulado, the voters were called by the beating of drums through the streets.

vened and when the Cortes met in 1837 the members of the
European provinces, usurping a power they did not possess,
refused admittance to the deputies from Cuba who at the
time published to the world a solemn and well grounded
protest. In framing the constitution then the assembly decreed
that the colonies should be governed by especial laws. These
facts have a paramount importance ; they show that the
grievances of Cuba cannot be laid to the Bourbons, and that
those who pretend that she has suffered alike with the rest
of the nation are sadly in error.

During these 32 years of usurpation of Cuba's rights, the
European provinces have managed to drain and crush the resources of that island for their exclusive benefit. They have
assumed the power of taxation and encouraged the Spanish
flag, repelling foreign trade and productions, and so constru-
ed the import duties as to take from the pockets of the
Cubans and fill those of the European producers.(a)

They have taken to themselves the decision of the local
matters of the islanders, and in order to meet with no obstacle in their selfish plan they have gradually taken from the
corporations and other boards the faculties these had exercised
of old, and appointed a bureaucratic structure thoroughly dependent on the administration and inimical to the rights of

(a) Marshal Serrano in his official report of the 10th of May, 1867, says : " we are forc-
" ed to acknowledge that in the last years the treasury of Cuba has been used abusively,
" which is partly the cause of the crisis the islands go through now and of the exhaustion
" of its resources."—

"The total expenditures for the departments of war and navy being 38½ millions of
"dollars, the Spanish Peninsula pays 25 and the islands 13½ millions ; can any argument
" prove that the Antilles with less than 2 millions of inhabitants should pay 35 per cent. and
" the metropolis with 15,673,000 only the remainder ?

" The state department of the kingdom costs 5 millions of dollars ; can it be just for Cuba
" to pay 2½ millions !"
(Report of the Commissioners.)

the Cuban citizen. Such has been the work of Spain under an uninterrupted enjoyment for herself of representative government.

In 1850 and 1854 filibustering expeditions were resorted to :—although started with Cuban funds, they were composed of Americans who were expected to produce the rising and could not be considered wholly Cuban like the present movement.

Some years later, the *intentions* of members of the Spanish government appearing to be that justice should be done to the colonies, a more hopeful and confiding feeling was awakened among the distinguished and enlightened men of Cuba.

Petitions and remonstrances were accordingly addressed; and the result was that in 1867, twenty-two commissioners elected from Cuba and Porto Rico met at Madrid, convened by the Metropolitan Government, to report on the law and institutions that Cuba desired.

Said report sets down the necessity of institutions like those of Canada : it decidedly advocates the emancipation of the slaves ; the voting of the taxes by the tax payers and a limited contribution of the islanders towards supporting the general government.

The facts I here bring to your mind bear so public a character and have transpired so markedly under our eye, that we are enabled to appreciate the justice of the cause, and the illegitimacy of the present rulers of Cuba.

When the provinces, now Republics of South America, attempted to throw off the Spanish yoke, there was no visible usurpation of acknowledged rights as in the present case.

I come to the last period :—the dynasty of Isabella 2d is set aside ; the sovereignty of the people proclaimed.

By one accord all the European provinces elect provincial

Juntas and free municipalities; (a) all Captain Generals holding
power from the Queen are removed, and it is further decreed
by the provisional government that where no substitute
should have been appointed the Captain General should resign unto the next in command.

And for Cuba what was done then?

The staunchest advocate of Queen Isabella, Gen. Lersundi,
a specimen of cynic vice and corruption was sustained, holding
unqualified authority.

A small band of Cubans started the revolution at the vil-
lage of *Yara*. The most eminent and distinguished citizens
of Havana, encouraged by their friends in Madrid, solicited of
Gen. Lersundi the participation in political life—similar existence to that enjoyed by the European provinces ; they
were insultingly spurned by the usurper from his palace, and
his conduct was subsequently approved by the Provisional
Government in Spain through the Duke de la Torre. (b)

After many days of anxiety Gen. Dulce arrived : the same
vessel brought an unusual number of greedy officials, some
too well known for immorality and corruption. Such was
the first gift of free Spain to her old and patient colony.(c)

Gen. Dulce, however, enjoyed the reputation of being a
Cuban liberal. He provoked long interviews with some
prominent men of Havana ; but no change was effected in
the municipalities, no Provincial Junta called, nothing to
assimilate Cuba to Spain, excepting the free press and the
permission for citizens to assemble, which lasted a few weeks
and was followed by the present reign of terror.

(a) To speak more correctly, these boards were in existence in Spain—and Cuba had
not before nor was she allowed to form them after the battle of Alcolea.

(b) See appendix No. 2.

(c) Perez Calvo, one of those appointed on this occasion, by the liberators of Spain, has
distinguished himself by his incendiary language and policy, marked by persecution, sequestration, bribery, until the volunteers, his tools and supporters, turned against him, and he
had to return to Spain.

During the short respite, meetings were held at the Marquis de Campo Florido's, where the most conservative gentlemen of Havana assisted private sessions, discussing what local government Cuba should have; and the result was quite similar to the report of the commissioners at Madrid in 1867.

Such being the record of the past, where should we look for the legitimate representation of the Island of Cuba now ?

To answer this question we must ascertain first, who Don Jose Morales Lemus is.

He is a man of talent and ability : his moral character stands unimpeached ; he is owner of considerable property. He has been the legal adviser of Europeans as well as Cubans. He has been manager of several Railroad and other companies, giving general satisfaction ; he was appointed member of the Council of Administration by the Government. Elected commissioner to the Junta which met at Madrid in 1867, to which I have alluded, he became the soul of the assembly, and his views and labors fill up the best part of the official report then issued.

At the dawn of the patriot movement, Morales Lemus appeared once more before the public, taking part in the debates at the house of the Marquis de Campo Florido, where the structure of the Provincial Government for Cuba was discussed, and he was the medium of elliciting a united vote from the distinguished proprietors of Havana, many of whom were European Spaniards.

The report submitted then to his supervision, and remodelled by him was unanimously approved.

With slight variations it looked to the same ends demanded by the commissioners in Madrid.

The next act of the drama just rapidly sketched finds Morales Lemus in the City of Washington, advocating the cause of Cuban independence and invested with powers from Carlos

Manuel de Cespedes, who is the avowed incarnation of the patriot-government of Cuba.

Can we hesitate in acknowledging Morales Lemus as a *more* legitimate representative of Cuba than the undisciplined soldiers foreign to the land they control by cruelty and force ?

As proof of the Spaniards' persistent resolution to usurp indefinitely unconstitutional power over Cuba, I judge proper to quote here, article 107 of the constitution just now submitted by the majority of the Cortes.

"The government of the provinces of Cuba and Porto "Rico shall be reformed as soon as the deputies from them "shall have taken seat at the Cortes, so as to extend to them, "with the modifications which may be thought necessary, "the rights set forth in the constitution."

Why do I address you these details, I believe it is unnecessary to say. I fear that masterly inactivity will not save that now fruitful island, nor American interest, and I believe that her resources are so great(a) that while alleviating the

(a) The statistics quoted officially by the Commissioners at Madrid in 1867, give the following items.

Gross products of country or agricultural capital	$124,225,318
Ditto of cattle raising estates	5,285,200
Ditto of City property	22,720,057
	$152,230,575

The Royal Decree of 12th Feb. 1867, establishing the income tax, sets down the net revenue of the wealth of Cuba as follows :

Net proceeds of rural property	$38,032,502.70
Ditto City ditto	17,040,043.34
Industry and commerce	77,384,649.65
Total Net Revenue	$132,457,195.69

Again in the same Royal Decree, article 16, it is affirmed that the net revenue of the rural and city property of Cuba amounts to $123,000,000, and in article 17 it is equally affirmed that the net profits of industry and commerce making what is judged a liberal deduction of 40 per cent. will come as high as 184,500,00

Hence the total Revenue would be $307,500,000

present burdens of taxation, Cuba can yet bear more than sufficient to pay back any sum, however large, that might be spent for her rescue. Nearly 32 millions of dollars in gold were assigned to her by the Metropolitan Government in the general budget last year, and forty millions have certainly been drawn through various channels up to this war.[a]

This *resume* of political usurpation, and other important facts can be confirmed by even the most conservative of the gentlemen now in the United States who have come flying from the indignities inflicted on them on their native soil. Even those who have publicly disavowed the insurrection cannot refuse their testimony to every assertion contained in this communication.

It is not for me to suggest any course, but were the Chief Magistrate of this Great Country only to express in a public document his abhorrence of the continued usurpation of rights, and the uncivilized and atrocious acts alluded to, such is the force of public opinion in this age, that the moral effect of such a manifestation would sink the hopes of the Spaniards and soon restore order and the regular course of business to that unhappy island.

(a) See appendix No. 3, 4 and 5.

APPENDIX No. 1.

Population of the island of Cuba according to General
Dulce's official report.

Whites.

Born in Spain and Canary
   Islands................115.114
Born in Cuba...........602.145
"   " Southern Repub-
lics and Brazil........... 4.203
Born in Europe(foreigners) 4.999
Resident Americans..... 2.496
                  —729.957=53.67 per cent.

Colored.

Free..................221.417
Slaves.................368.550
Captured Emancipados.. 4.521
            ——— 594.488=43.67 per cent.
Asiatic and Yucatese   34.793= 2.66 per cent.

              1.359.238= 100.

Census as published by Fernandez Corredor.

White residents........730.894
Foreign ditto 5.298
Transient Spanish and
   Foreign 21.420
Chinese 34.825
Yucatese.............. 1.047

                          793.484

```
Forward, ............................................793,484
Free Colored and Eman-
    cipados, males ...... 113.806
Females ...............118.687
                       ————            232.493
Slaves, males..........218.722
   "    females........151.831        370.553
                       ————            ————       503.045
                                                  ————
                                       Total,  1.396.530
```

N. B.—Of the slaves only 172,671 are employed on sugar estates.

APPENDIX No. 2.

Memorandum of the Incidents of a Meeting held at General Lersundi's Palace, of several respectable and wealthy citizens of Havana, on the 24th October, 1868.

The telegraphic news of revolutionary movements in Spain was naturally sympathized with by a majority of the people in Cuba, whose sentiments are decidedly liberal; and the principles there proclaimed deeply agitated the public mind, inspiring the wish to participate in similar advantages. The desire was evident to obtain a guaranty, an assurance or a direct promise that the island was not to be cut off as before from the national progress, nor its inhabitants despoiled of the rights of Spanish citizens, much less be left under the imputation of being obdurate partizans of the fallen dynasty. The desired promise not being made, nor the guaranty obtained, fears were entertained as to the policy contemplated, and many suspected that Cubans would not be allowed the exercise of the rights acknowledged for the rest of the nation ; and not a few imagined that in the incipient stage of the revolution, a decree might be received from the metropolis ordering the sudden abolition of slavery, thereby imperiling the social existence of the country. It is proper to add that this last idea was artfully suggested by the enemies of free institutions, with a view to preserve the *regime* of Isabel in these distant regions.

Notwithstanding the efforts made to keep order and peace, the masses were excited and a rising took place far away from the capital, the leaders yet invoking in their war cry, "Spain, Cuba, and Freedom !"

Thus, expectancy, anxious doubts and alarming fears produced an extraordinary and undescribable situation, while the impatient could not be restrained and would claim what they feared would be denied, the over cautious little pleased with the glorious revolution of Spain, were a subject of annoyance to the former, who in them saw a powerful obstacle to their aspirations—addresses were therefore made by one party to maintain *statu quo*, while the other rose in arms, the last resort of the oppressed nations. Hence originated the thought of allowing a certain expansion by frank adherence to the principles of the Provisional Government of Madrid. * *

* * * * * * * * * *

On Friday, 23d October, Messieurs Rato, Zulueta, Pelligero, Fernandez Bramosio, Mestre, and other aldermen, were discussing the subject in an extra official and friendly manner in the recess-room of the city council of Havana. It was generally granted that meetings of citizens should be authorized by the Government to soothe public anxiety, quell disturbances, and discuss the slavery question ; a few hours later invitations were received to a meeting at the Captain General's palace. The gentlemen mentioned at the bottom of this memorandum, and others whose names are not remembered, appeared on the 24th October at the palace, and were shown into the private apartment of Lersundi, who in a tone of evident displeasure, said he had no idea the meeting was to be so large, but since it was so, they could pass into the parlor, where there would be room for all. Once there, he said he had been told that several residents desired to address him, he had agreed to hear them and though not expecting so many, the number only added to the honor and pleasure with which he ought to hear them.

These remarks were calculated to embarass the invited party, who had come to hear the suggestions of the Government rather than to initiate the subject themselves, and a profound silence followed. This being noticed by Lersundi, he required Rato, who had been one of those proposing the invitation, to state the object of. the meeting.

Senor Rato said, that in the grave circumstances the island was going through, several persons had wished to express to the Captain General sentiments of adhesion and personal respect. Lersundi seemed disposed then to hear others.

Senor Mestre then spoke : He said that his individuality was of little account, and that he should rather be the last than the first to speak, but the remarks of Senor Rato forced him to precede gentlemen with better right to take part in the conference ; he would speak in perfect frankness, because there are moments when all should be frankly told ; he had conversed with Senor Rato and others, to the purpose that it was expedient to authorize or tolerate meetings for the discussion of public matters interesting to all, and therefore he thought it incumbent on him to make certain explanations ; he said the serious events happening in Spain had produced excitement and trouble easy to understand ; the Government in power having proclaimed the most advanced political creed, every Spaniard, no matter in what part of the world he found himself, should feel he was entitled to the enjoyment of the acknowledged rights of the revolution, therefore the inhabitants of Cuba could but believe that they would be extended to this province as an integral part of the nation ; he would ask what should be done ? We should doubtless adopt an open and decidedly liberal course in harmony with the established and legal regime of the Peninsula. He said that the meetings he had referred to were expedient as well as to give greater scope to the press, in order to furnish public sentiment with safety valves ; that when these were closed the expansion would burst through clandestine issues, the danger of which it was needless to explain. He enjoined to take care that no disunion should ever exist between the property holders and the advocates of advanced freedom ; that the latter should never notice disagreement between these two elements, which would cause great mischief. By the means he proposed, a proper expansion of feeling within reasonable bounds, would be harmless and important changes would be accomplished with no danger ; he said the most liberal policy should be held as the most conservative ; this was the motive for asking meetings ; he thought it calculated to prevent present as well as future evils; at these meetings honest and patriotic men would investigate the serious points now pending, would infuse a spirit of unity and carry to the furthest ends of the province, hope and a feeling of security in the future, and thereby exercise a salutary influence all around.

Senor Modet (a) said he adhered to all the remarks of Senor Mestre ; he said that as member of the Cortes, he had advocated the extension of political rights to the inhabitants of Cuba, and Porto Rico; in his opinion the country would become quiet if the legitimate hope were in any way expressed that this Province would be assimilated to those of Spain, that the liberties gloriously conquered would be enjoyed here, since it was known from reliable accounts that a provisional Government existed in Madrid accepted by all the provinces, although temporary in its character ; he said that by such means union, tranquility, confidence, and order among the inhabitants of Cuba, would be established. Should a doubt arise as to the proper course, he proposed the home Government to be consulted by telegraph.

The Captain General then suspended the conference, saying, he had understood that some residents desired to offer

(a)This gentleman, a native of Spain and Col. of engineers, was sent to Spain by Lersundi, in consequence of this speech ; he returned under Dulce, and has now been sent back, frightened away by the volunteers.

him their support, and found on the contrary that they had come only to show mistrust, to censure his acts and address him charges to which he would briefly refer. It had been insinuated that the revolution had acknowledged certain rights to all Spaniards—that persons having constituted a provisional government at Madrid desired to make those rights extensive to this island ; that some one was in the way between the mother country and this province, and that such party was himself. For his part he had received no direct communications from that government, not even by telegraph, excepting one from the new minister of the colonies, which had been published entire by his order. What else could he do in favor of the island in the fulfillment of his duty than overlook his own personal views and sympathies? He would obey orders that might arrive from the Madrid Government, the government, he added of the Duke de La Torre, the government of General Serrano. He was determined to resign his command when the time came, handing over the island in the condition he had received it. But he would in no way express adhesion, as would be intimated by the gentlemen who had spoken, because his loyalty rose as high as the throne of God. He said the remarks of Senor Mestre were analogous to those made by the insurgents of Yara in arms, whose conduct he seemed to excuse, he said that such had been the commencement of insurrections in the Spanish countries now republics in America. He discussed these topics at large and stating that the goverment counted on means adequate to suppress and punish the rebels and agitators, he remarked that the answer he had thought proper to give Messrs. Mestre and Modet being ended, he would close the conference which ought by no means to be held longer.

Senor Modet asked to be allowed to speak and was refused.

The vehemence of gesture, tone of voice, and unexpected severity of Lersundi, naturally left a most disagreeable impression on all present. They began to retire with evident discontent when Senor Morales Lemus told the Captain General how much he regretted that his excellency should have interpreted as accusations the suggestions made with the best intentions ; the General insisted on the impropriety of the meetings asked for, saying, it would be more useful if the newspaper, *El Pais*, (a) should pointedly and energetically condemn the movement of the insurgents, or if two commissioners were sent to obtain their surrender. His experience taught him that no convictions were ever gained by debating. Sometimes, he added, as it were casually, it is unquestionable that timely severity produced the best results ; the sacrifice of a few lives at a proper movement, will save from greater and more painful losses.

Those yet remaining at the palace departed after this effusion, and thus ended a scene initiated under favorable auspices which might have exercised a beneficial influence on the destinies of Cuba. This new page of its history needs no comment.

Names of those known to have been present :

Conde Canongo,	Nicolas Martinez Valdivieso,
Apolinar Rato,	Domingo Guillermo Arozarena
Manuel de Armas,	Jose Ruiz de Leon,
Conde San Ignacio,	Juan Poey,
Jose Morales Lemus,	Nicanor Troncoso,
Julian Zulueta,	Miguel Antonio Herrera,
Antonio Fernandez Bramosio	Hilario Cisneros,
Francisco Ibanez,	Juan Ariza,

(a.) El Pais. organ of the Cubans.

Pedro Martin Rivero,
Eduardo Alonso Colmenares,
Conde Pozos-Dulces,
Jose Suarez Argudin,
Jose Manuel Mestre,
Juan Modet,
Gonzalo Jorrin,
Ramon Herrera,
Marques Aguas-Claras,
Jose Villasante,
Jose M. Morales Cerro,

Antonio Gonzalez Mendoza,
Francisco Duran Cuervo,
Adolfo Munoz,
Sabino Ojero,
Francisco Acosta,
Jose Pelligero de Lama,
Enrique Farres,
Jose Antonio Echeverria,
Pedro Sotolongo,
Jose Caraza,
Antonio Mora.

APPENDIX No. 3.

Table of products of the Island of Cuba, from the semi-official statistics, by Don Francisco Fernandez Corredor :

63,380 houses, annual rent,	$16,260,060
3,285 cattle haciendas, 270,798 bullocks and cows, 35,200 horses and mares, 3,342 mules and asses, 349.960 hogs, 34,813 sheep and goats,	5,286,180
1,365 sugar estates, prod'g 1,127,351,750 lbs. with molasses, rum, and savings attached to the culture,	67,641,105
996 coffee estates, producing 16,822,000 lbs.	2,523,300
9,482 vegas of tobacco, prod'g 69,030,000 lbs.	16,912,500
Wax, 5,227,600 lbs.	1,794,384
Honey, 362,276 barrels,	1,266,966
5,738' pasture grounds, and 21,842 farms, pro'g 4,902,525 lbs. cocoa, 500.000 " cotton, 125.000 " arrowroot, 50,000,000 " rice, 7,329,425 " beans, 7,500,000 " potatoes, 1,025 " indigo, 2,000,000 " seroons of plantains, 2,192,775 " cheese, 125,000,000 nourishing roots or vegetables, 70,000 loads of greens. 1,000,000 " maloja, or corn grn. fodder, 240,000,000 lbs. of corn,	13,748,746
Ginger, Palm Leaf, rope bark (majagua) bituminous coal, (chapapote),	1.000,000
Fruits, milk, starch, poultry & eggs, 3,836,866 Brick manufactures, block quarries, 1,419,000 Timber, 1.380,000 Fisheries 1,000,000 Copper ore, 984,587	
	$8,620,453
	$135,053,694

Forward, ... $135,053,694

106,088 separate estates, urban or rustic,
20,156 establishments of industry and commerce ; anonymous companies, professions, arts and trades, . 124,469,117

Total amount of products & annual incomes, $259,522,811

APPENDIX No. 4.

Amount of the Territorial tax on net income avowed by the corporations for the fiscal year of 1868–1869.

REVENUE.

City,_____28,679,800
Rural, _____90,152,400
_____
118,832,200

10 per cent. ordered by the decree of 12th
Feb'y, 1867, . . . $11,883,220

N. B. This tax has been since raised to over 14 per cent., besides the return to high import duties which were reduced when the above-mentioned decree was first issued. In March $1 per ton was exacted on the exportation of Sugar; in April it was raised to $1.38, and similar duties on Segars, Tobacco, &c. We may safely calculate that for the fiscal year to end in July, 1870, the Spanish rulers intend to draw from the private revenue of the people of Cuba, not less than from fifty to sixty millions of dollars, with no heed of the misery and ruin thereby created.

APPENDIX No. 5.

Area of the island of Cuba as described by General Dulce, in the Report of 1867 :

Cuba contains 639,777 cavaleries of land, or 21,112,641 acres apportioned as follows :

Under cultivation, .	14.59 per cent.
Pastures, ...	27.50	"
Mineral appropriated, .	0.69	"
Wood lands, . .	39.72	"
Barren, .	. 17.50	"

_____
100.00

In printing the following Report of Marshal Serrano, Duke de la Torre, ex-Captain General of Cuba and present Regent of Spain, the translator has a two-fold object in view: to show, on the one hand, by the testimony of such unquestionable authority, that the struggling Cuban patriots have neither falsely arraigned their task-masters, nor overstated the grinding tyranny to which Spain subjects their unhappy island: and on the other to dispel an illusion under which many worthy citizens seem to labor,—that Cuban oppression was the crime of the Monarchy; and that the advent of the people to power will bring amelioration to the political condition of that Antille.

But who that is at the pain of wading through the turgid pages of the ex-Captain-General, written with an experimental knowledge of his subject, and reflects that it is the same Serrano,—thus feeling and thus writing but two short years ago,—that to-day, as the representative of the Spanish *people*, joins hands with Lersundi, the most ruthless and cynic of the petty instruments of spoliation, employed by the avaricious monarchs of Spain—joins hands to insult the hopes by him so lately excited, and crush with despotic heel the aspirations he but yesterday boasted of inspiring. Who, we ask, reading this Report and reflecting on the present situation, can continue under the illusion.

No, unhappy Cuba has nothing to hope, either from the avarice of Spanish monarchs, or cupidity of the Spanish people:—and so thinking and so believing, the Antillians, after weary years of patient waiting, have heroically drawn the sword and cast away the scabbard,—invoking the sympathy of all liberty-loving peoples, and referring their cause to the dread arbitrament of the God of battles.

In the presence of such a conflict what American will not join the cry :

Down with the Spaniard's hated flag,
To FREEDOM baneful sight:
Fling Cuba's Lone Star to the breeze,
And GOD DEFEND THE RIGHT.

J. R. R.......

REPORT

OF

MARSHAL SERRANO,

DUKE DE LA TORRE, (PRESENT REGENT OF SPAIN,)

ON THE

INTERROGATORIES SUBMITTED TO HIM

BY THE

SPANISH GOVERNMENT,

IN THE MATTER OF REFORM IN THE REGIME OF THE ANTILLES.

(TRANSLATED FROM THE SPANISH.)

Owing to personal considerations I am obliged to give a simultaneous answer to the three questions addressed to me under successive dates by your Excellency's cabinet, in reference to the royal decree of 25th of November, 1865, ordering an investigation for the purpose of ascertaining the reforms demanded by the necessities and wishes of the colonies.

This circumstance, though foreign to the report, facilitates my task, because, from my official character, it does not become me to enter into certain details that must have been sufficiently illustrated by the Commissioners elected from the islands of Cuba and Porto-Rico. Including in one answer the several points relative to the three questions, I am enabled to be more laconic and clear in developing ideas, which are, however, well known in Spain, where I never made a mystery of them. The subject of reform in the "regime" of the Antilles, is not a party question, it is a national one; and as to myself, I never have or shall judge otherwise, than as a

Spaniard loving his country and race and ardently desiring to strengthen and perpetuate the union between those distant provinces and the mother country: for, I find not only great advantage to the nation in holding rich and flourishing provinces, but also in assuring thereby a basis to the influence that Spain cannot fail to exercise in the future, however long may be the duration, and far off the end of the present struggle in the vast extent of the American Continent where the Castilian language is spoken.

The report embraces three essential points :

1st. The basis on which the special laws should be founded in carrying out Art. 80 of the Constitution of the Spanish Monarchy, to be presented to the Cortes for the government of Cuba and Porto-Rico.

2d. The making of such treaties of navigation and commerce with other nations as may be found expedient; and such changes in the tariff and custom-house regulations of these islands as may be necessary for their execution.

3rd. Manner of organizing the labor of the colored and Asiatic population, and of promoting such immigration as may be considered most favorable to those provinces.

I.

I shall commence by observing, that as I have exercised during a period of more than three years the supreme political and military command in the island of Cuba, to this island I shall more particularly refer in my observations; although I consider them equally applicable to Porto-Rico, both Antilles being with few exceptions in the same condition.

Spanish dominion in America, though not free from the abuses history records, nevertheless evinces an earnest disposition on the part of Spanish monarchs to equalize, as far as possible, the condition of the conquered countries with that of Castile and Leon ; a disposition frequently manifested in checking the avarice and excesses of some of the conquerors.

That spirit, as the exposition that preceeds the royal decree of the 27th of July, 1859, concerning municipalities in the island of Cuba correctly states, is a traditional rule of the monarchy since the time of the invincible Emperor, Charles the 1st, and which is preserved in various decrees of Don Felipe 2d, Don Felipe 4th, and in those for the observance of the Intendentes dictated for New Spain, by the king, Don Carlos 3rd, of grateful memory ;—has inspired all the laws of the Indies, and will always be one of the historic glories of our country. The text of the law 13, title 2d, book 2d, of that venerable code, is as follows :

" The kingdoms of Castille and the Indies, belonging to one crown, the laws and structure of government of each should be as similar and harmonious as possible. And our council should endeavor that the laws and decrees issued for the government of the Indies, be made to assimilate as nearly as possible, considering the variety and difference of countries and people, to those prevailing in Castile and Leon."

The assimilating precept of the law of the Indies, was endeavored to be applied constantly in the government of the American colonies during the period of absolute rule, and in conformity to it the Spanish nation, when, in the beginning of the present century, the Cortes of Cadiz met on the basis of a representative system, called the deputies from America; and they continued to hold in all the Cortes until 1836, the same representation as the provinces of the Peninsula and the adjacent islands. The legislators of these last decided not to admit in Congress the deputies from the colonies ; and afterwards provided in an additional article of the Constitution of 1837 (repeated in Art. 80 of that of 1845), that such provinces should be governed by special laws.

Undoubtedly it was intended in 1836, to deprive the Antilles of representation in the Cortes; and that desire shared by many, either through the false belief, already disproved by history, that the deputies from America, inspired with their passionate discourses, the people from whence they proceeded with ideas of independence; or through the fear that the American deputies might draw the attention of Congress from subjects of national interest. By others this action was justified on the ground of the great distance that separated the Antilles from the mother country, and the convenience of their exercising political rights in an autonomic form without representative ties to the home government, like England's system with her colonies in America and Australia.

No one now denies that the spirit of independence gained strength on the American continent many years previous to its having sent deputies to the Cortes of Cadiz; and it is clear that once on that road the hazardous circumstances in which the war of Independence placed the mother country, had the effect of precipitating in their march the Continental provinces of America. On that account, and because the state of revolution in which they actually were, provoked repressive measures in its interior government, all of which constituted an abnormal situation, and explains why their deputies appeared to a certain degree animated by the reigning spirit of the revolted people. Neither, without violence, is it possible to ascribe to cause what was effect : nor was this spirit of the deputies from Continental America, shared by the deputies from the Antilles, who, on the contrary, were ever seen promoting discussions of real practical interest. Neither did the fever for independence ever pass through Cuba and Porto-Rico, the inhabitants of which lent their spontaneous aid to the mother country in men and money ; not only for the glorious campaign of independence, but also for the most disastrous and lamentable civil war with which, at the cost of so much Spanish blood, the nation, including the Antilles, has conquered the right to be constitutionally governed.

Besides, if the influence in Congress of the American deputies, was such as to excite apprehension when the domains of Spain in the New World, surpassed the Peninsula both in population and territory, such sectional influence is no longer to be dreaded, as the American provinces are reduced to the islands of Cuba and Porto-Rico, and the distance, thanks to the new and easier communications, shortened since 1836, and still continuing to be diminished.

And as to the danger that the deputies from the Antilles may inflame their compatriots with ideas of independence, I am convinced that the great majority of their inhabitants do not believe in the islands of Cuba and Porto-Rico, possessing the necessary elements for constituting themselves as independent nations; and this affords an explanation of the tendency to annexation to the United States, which fortunately has appeared at various intervals in the island of Cuba. I say fortunately, because that tendency of seeking liberty in the folds of a people of another race, different habits and language, could never be and never has been popular in Cuba, where annexation attempts have always failed, as singnally shown in the want of support by the country of the two Lopez expeditions.

Therefore, I should more fear the discontent springing from the humiliation with which the actual regime offends the pride of our race, that has not degenerated in the people of Cuba and Porto-Rico, might lead them to measures not less ruinous to the Antilles than dangerous to our domination in America; but I firmly believe that a government in which those Spanish islanders should be duly represented as they have a right to be, would perpetuate their union with the mother-country: and I by no means believe the English colonial system applicable to our American provinces, because under that system the colonies do not contribute to the support of the nation, and consequently have not as much right to be represented in the Supreme Goverment of the mother-country, as the islands of Cuba and Porto-Rico, which, in the form of a surplus revenue, or by some means that best determines their just co-operation, contributes, and should continue to contribute, because they can do so, to the expenses of the mother-country.

I have gone through the above observations so as to demonstrate that some of the appreciations that may have inspired the legislators of 1837, being mistaken, the motives of many others having disappeared, and under the present circumstances, the representation in the Cortes of the islands of Cuba and Porto-Rico, does not offer the least obstacle, and will satisfy the just and universal cry from those islands—more so since the hope of obtaining it has awakened itself in the mind of its people. And this naturally carries me back to the personal experience I was able to acquire, whilst in command of the island of Cuba.

Having been preceded in the command by the worthy Lieutenant-General, Marquis de la Habana, who was appointed to discharge it during times of great danger, and having great satisfaction to acknowledge and proclaim here, that General Concha knew how to confront them, not only because he discovered, but thwarted the great annexation conspiracy that was to have started in the first months of 1855, but on account of the many and important administrative reforms he initiated and was able to carry out during his second above mentioned command, and succeeded in a great measure in calming the deep and general discontent, and by turning the eyes of the disaffected to the mother-country, encouraged them to hope for justice from her, dissuaded them from violence, and an attempt at change of nationality, a change always involving painful sacrifice.

The agreement of the Cortes of 1836 and the constitutional precept of 1837, practically carried out, though of different meaning, by denying to the natives of the Antilles all political rights; the stringent measures so exaggerated by the local government of the island of Cuba, and the fearful administrative chaos which followed that period and which my predecessor, the Marquis de la Habana, has so graphically depicted in two printed memoires, brought to its highest point the general discontent in the island; while at the same time complete anarchy prevailed throughout the South American Republics; and on the other hand the flourishing and advancing condition of the United States brought about a desire for annexation, a desire supported by the tendency of that country towards territorial aggrandizement in Mexico; and this called out a real annexation party.

The news of the French Revolutions of 1848, reached Cuba, simultaneously with that of the provisional government having decreed the immediate abolition of slavery in the colonies, and it was feared by many, that an analogous convulsion in Spain might produce the same results: this apprehension induced many proprietors to join the annexationist, as they saw the existence of slavery in the democratic and liberal form of their constitution.

This accounts for the financial resources that the annexation party always counted on; and certainly if they could have had the support and sympathies of all the Cuban people, there is no doubt that a pretext for armed intervention by the United States, would soon have sprung up, and Cuba would have been lost to Spain.

Fortunately as I have already said, the sympathies of the Cuban people were not with the annexationists, as was well proved by the energetic opposition with which it was repudiated by Don Jose Antonio Saco, and other writers of the same Antille; and as was shown more so in the powerless state and the complete abstention in seconding the two invasions of Cardenas and Las Pozas under General Lopez.

The annexation party lost no time notwithstanding; on the contrary, encouraged by instigations even from the government of the United States, with resources of money and with the direction in the country of a Spaniard from the Peninsula, gifted with notable qualities of character and enlightment, organized a formidable conspiracy in the interior of the island; while in the United States an equally formidable expedition under General Quitman, was preparing to land in Cuba in the early part of the year, 1855.

This double danger having passed away, and the passions excited thereby quieted, the mind of Cuba quietly prepared itself for that truly great and national movement, which under the name of the reform party, gathered round it all those who with hopes such as I and many others in our character as true Spaniards, have thought that we ought to encourage, and which, according to my judgment, ought not to be overlooked by the patriotism of the government. There is a reaction favorable to Spanish nationality, which I think I succeeded in inspiring and developing during my command, which calls for political equality with the other Spanish provinces. A demand founded on such incontestible justice, unless recklessly despised, assures to us the perpetual union of the two Spanish Antilles. For they cannot and do not wish to be independent and will never accept without violence and without painful sacrifice, annexation to the United States. But they demand a liberal representative government, and will not consent to be deprived of the advantages and guarantees which such government affords.

It seems to me that I understand well the actual tendencies of the Cubans ; I endeavored to gain their friendship and to listen with impartiality to their complaints and aspirations; I succeeded in deserving the first, I say it with satisfaction, and even after I left Havana, I have kept up a constant correspondence with many of their most important men, having among others received a letter of a public character, in which they express their wishes, and which is signed by Cubans of notoriety from all parts of the island. I cannot but say to the government of Her Majesty, influenced by the loyalty of my character and the most sincere conviction, that the grievances of the Cubans are just, that their aspirations are lawful, that there is no reason why, Spaniards like ourselves, they should not have a free press, nor a proper representation in government, and all those constitutional guaranties to which the Spaniards of the Peninsula have a right ; that there is no reason why a military and absolute government from the highest to the lowest grades in the scale, should be the only regime for the Antilles; and that the moment has now precisely arrived, let not the government forget it, to take advantage of the internal and external circumstances which favor political reform, urgently demanded by the Spaniards of the Antilles, and which it is just and prudent to grant without delay.

I have said internal circumstances, because, had the political reform been made when asked of the Constitutional Cortes in 1855, many notable men of those who figure in Havana in the Spanish party, the same who have come out opposed to it, after the Spanish tendency of the liberal aspirations of the Cubans has removed from them the fear of annexation of Cuba to the United States, which the recent discovery of the conspiracy of that year yet inspired them,— had the reforms then been granted, it would, perhaps, have appeared as an act of weakness in the metropolis, and not as an act of premeditated justice ; but now that the party for annexation no longer exists; now that the only active Cuban party aspires to the exercise of political rights under the dependence of Spain, to-day it is that a prudent and foreseeing government can make such ample concessions to the Antilles, as will assure to us forever their possession. Likewise the external circumstances are favorable, on account of the late war in the United States, that has destroyed the bonds of sympathy that linked the pro-slavery minds, by the abolition of that institution, and on the other hand, exacting from their Government all its attention for several years to its own reconstruction, completely allows the Spanish nation to be generous in its concessions of justice,—and this before new complications erect barriers that may embarass them.

I cannot believe that the Consulting Council, which is indicated in the third question of the Political Interrogatory, can satisfy either Cubans or Porto-Riqueans, who desire to be represented in Government in the same way the other provinces of the monarchy are ; and as these aspirations are more on account of their dignity than convenience, without ignoring the advantages that the Government would acquire from persons well acquainted with the subject, and especial interest and opinions in the Antilles, I believe that their representation in the Spanish Congress not only offers this advantage, but satisfies also, without the slightest danger to the Metropolis, the sentiment of dignity amongst the Cubans, and Porto-Riqueans, who are not satisfied with being less than the other Spaniards. I therefore believe that their admittance to the Cortes is not only an act of justice, but of the highest national convenience.

The basis of this representation should be the same, in proportion to free inhabitants, as obtains in the peninsula : and as to the electoral qualification, I confess I do not perceive the least danger from placing it on a similar footing; calculating the silver reals as reals de vellon, our standard here, giving the electoral franchise to those only who pay at least twenty-five dollars in direct taxes.

And the Government should avoid those artifices of the present municipal laws, which seek the election of as many peninsulers as islanders. They but serve to provoke provincial animosities.

If not 25, let 50 dollars be the regulating standard for the right to vote ; though I must again repeat that there is not the slightest danger in the first. But by no means must the hopes be crushed of the acquisition of a complete equality with the Peninsula. Let the distinction of classes be at once suppressed, and the amount of taxes paid, regardless of their source, and not even excepting the professions, be the only standard.

As to the interior regime of the island of Cuba, the proper diffusion of political power over its extended territory and the prevention of a centralization which would work injuriously to all interests, require its division into several provinces. The island was once divided into three, and I think I have heard of this division having recently been reestablished ; but it appears to me, and this view has been confirmed by several distinguished Cubans, that the increased population would justify its division into six provinces, namely : Havana, Pinar del Rio, Matanzas, Villaclara, Puerto-Principe and St. Jago de Cuba.

According to the law of the Indies already mentioned, there can be no obstacle to the organization of these provinces upon the same footing as obtains in the Peninsula, with their Deputations and Provincial Councils : but were the first elected in accordance with the electoral law that may be established for the deputies to the Cortes, and the second named by the Superior Governor, it would bring inconvenience at once perceptible.

Each Province should have its Governor without the military command, just as in the Peninsula, and in order to assure the appointment of persons well informed of the country's wants and interest, it would be undoubtedly best to have them appointed, or at least proposed, by the Superior Governor.

The existence of a Superior Governor, to represent the executive and initiatory power in all affairs of local interest, and to exercise surveillance over the Governors of Provinces, as is done by the Supreme Government on the Peninsula, is, in my opinion, indispensable. And he should possess that amplitude of authority and means that our Viceroys and Captains-General have always possessed, to the end that all matters simply local, and in no way affecting national interests, such as anonymous socities, railway concessions, instruction, public works and the like, be acted upon by him, thereby avoiding the loss of time, and saving the expense incident to their reference to the Home Government.

It being well understood that their provisional execution by the Superior Governor should be without prejudice to the final approval or disapproval of the Supreme Government. Formerly, the Reales Acuerdos (high Courts acting as Government council) in the exercise of these faculties, modified the authority of the Viceroys or Captain-Generals. The progress of administrative science made it clear later, that the government attributions were incompatible with those of the judiciary and in Havana, in order to substitute them, a council of administration was formed, which does not correspond to the necessities of the representative system and which should be essentially modified when the political organization of the administration will have been reformed in the island.

What, in my judgment, seems most reasonable is, that as there would be a " Provincial Deputation" there should also be an " Insular Deputation," sharing the initiative with the Superior Civil Governor in all questions of general and especial interest to the island.

Moreover, and in order that the executive may not be subjected to the electoral power, another insular body might be established similar to the Council of the Provinces—in the appointment of whose members the Superior Governor would take part.

As a guarantee of success it should be provided that all questions peculiar to the island should be initiated by either the Superior Governor, the Insular Counsel or Insular Deputations, and no such Decree be executed without their triple approbation—subject, however, to the approval or disapproval of the Supreme Government. In regard to which latter it would be well to fix a term, say a year, at the expiration of which the Supreme Government, not having expressed its disapprobation, it would be understood that the decrees of the Superior Governor, in cord with the two insular bodies, would be considered valid.

To dissipate the want of confidence engendered in the minds of the tax payers by the long course of abuses which has prevailed—a truthful and calm discussion of the budget of the Antilles is absolutely necessary to scure the acquiescence of those to be affected by it.

To confound this Budget with the general one of the Peninsula, would be an error of the most fatal consequences, both to the mother country and to the ultramarine provinces, because the peculiar condition of the provinces call for, and will for a long time demand, a special mode of tax-paying. What appears, therefore, most convenient and appropriate, is the subdivision of the Budget, leaving to the insular deputation, the definite approval of a peculiar and exclusive one for the island, sufficient to provide for the wants of its interior administration: and should be stipulated by the Superior Governor; the Supreme Government reserving to itself the appointment of certain salaries of high officials, in the proportionate rule that may seem most adequate; and the assignment of the share which each of the Antilles should contribute towards the national expenses, so that this share may be in proportion to that of the other provinces; and neither this share, nor these above-mentioned salaries, should be discussed but in the Cortes, where the Antilles will have their representation and deputies.

As regards municipalities, the same rule ought at once to be applied both to Cuba and Porto-Rico, as to their organization and attributes, that is observed in the Peninsula:

though it appears to me quite unnecessary that the Government should reserve to itself the appointment of the mayors.

I would leave the municipal Alcaldes as sole government authorities where no governors exist ; and I would also confer on Lieutenant Alcaldes the government of villages without municipalities, which may be members of the nearest municipal corporations ; in this way superceding ' the military Lieutenant-Governors and Captains-Pedaneos with great advantage to the morality of the administration, and ⁻

The matter of the Budget of the Antilles, which is the principal basis of representation, is one especially calling for the consideration of the Government. We are bound to acknowledge that in the last years the treasury of Cuba has been used abusively, which is partly the cause of the crisis the islands are now going through ; and of the exhaustion of the resources of the treasury.

This paragraph having been accidentally omitted by the printer, we consider too important—as an admission by the author of the proper basis of representation, and the abuses of treasury management—to be left out.—TR.

politically and in the representative form, the government of the islands of Cuba and Porto Rico, and in this way the real spirit of the laws of the Indies would not only be observed, but a general satisfaction be diffused among most worthy Spaniards who aspire to be our brothers, an appellation which, while the actual law denies them any participation in making those by which they are governed, is truly irony.

In the present state of civilization, we cannot conceive any country resigning itself to be governed by an absolute power, and still less can we conceive that any province should resign

As a guarantee of success it should be provided that all
questions

. . . . and, a special mode of tax-paying.
What appears, therefore, most convenient and appropriate, is
the subdivision of the Budget, leaving to the insular deputation, the definite approval of a peculiar and exclusive one
for the island, sufficient to provide for the wants of its interior
administration: and should be stipulated by the Superior
Governor; the Supreme Government reserving to itself the
appointment of certain salaries of high officials, in the proportionate rule that may seem most adequate; and the
assignment of the share which each of the Antilles
should contribute towards the national expenses, so that this
share may be in proportion to that of the other provinces;
and neither this share, nor these above-mentioned salaries,
should be discussed but in the Cortes, where the Antilles
will have their representation and deputies.

As regards municipalities, the same rule ought at once to
be applied both to Cuba and Porto-Rico, as to their organization and attributes, that is observed in the Peninsula:

though it appears to me quite unnecessary that the Government should reserve to itself the appointment of the mayors.

I would leave the municipal Alcaldes as sole government authorities where no governors exist ; and I would also confer on Lieutenant Alcaldes the government of villages without municipalities, which may be members of the nearest municipal corporations ; in this way superceding ' the military Lieutenant-Governors and Captains-Pedaneos with great advantage to the morality of the administration, and the encouragement of the growth of small villages.

As to the press, I see no reason why the same rule that is established on the Peninsula should not be established in the Antilles. I doubt not there being different political opinions there, because wherever men that think can be found, there will necessarily exist diversity of ideas ; but correctly speaking, political parties and passions that excite to contest between each other, cannot be conceived where the supreme executive power does not reside, and as the insular press can never have the pretension of overthrowing ministries, there will be a cause less for public opinion and order to be disturbed.

To the limits assigned to the press in Spain, respecting the King and the Catholic religion, might be added in the Antilles, the obligation of respecting slavery also, whilst this institution legally exists.

Such are the bases on which, in conformity with the true principles of justice, the fulfilment of the Article 80 of the Constitution of the Monarchy should rest, in organizing politically and in the representative form, the government of the islands of Cuba and Porto Rico, and in this way the real spirit of the laws of the Indies would not only be observed, but a general satisfaction be diffused among most worthy Spaniards who aspire to be our brothers, an appellation which, while the actual law denies them any participation in making those by which they are governed, is truly irony.

In the present state of civilization, we cannot conceive any country resigning itself to be governed by an absolute power, and still less can we conceive that any province should resign sentation of her sister provinces, for here there is not only the want of guarantees and securities that exist under an absolute regime, but the humiliation of being placed under people of the same country.

Let this most important consideration not be overlooked by Her Majesty's ministers, on whom the honor may fall to carry out to a successful end the great national enterprise of conquering for the mother Spain, through a just and liberal political reform, the hearts and good wishes of all Spanish Antillians.

All that I have so far said in the present Report answers the first nine questions of the Political Interrogatory. The tenth inquires into the degree of participation which should be given in political rights to free colored persons ; and limiting myself, in this most arduous and serious question, to place before Government two considerations, in my opinion equally worthy of attention. I will end by pointing out the convenience of the solution of the question being left to the decision of the Superior Government of the islands, jointly with the Insular Corporations already referred to. These two are : on one side, the necessity of respecting the customs thar the institution of slavery must have created in the Antilles, establishing social hierarchy between the white and black race ; and on the other, the danger that would arise from establishing between the races visible legal divisions, creating the greatest obstacles in the political participation of the free colored men ; an agreement must be sought for, and on this agreement it is desirable the parties directly interested should be consulted.

II.

Without going into details of the financial question, that is largely embraced in the second interrogatory, I will say that I consider the Budget of the Island of Cuba susceptible of great economies ; that whatever change takes place in the tax-paying, special care be taken that a country so long un-

equally governed should not be discontented ; that the
United States, being her natural market, and where is con-
sumed at least one-half of her sugar produce, the Government
should always incline itself towards favoring the commercial
relations between the great Antille and her natural market ;
that Spain is bound to clear the way for the produce of the
Antilles that now go to the United States, and other countries in Europe, on account of the obstacles they find here in
the heavy import duties on sugar, and in the tobacco monopoly, at the same time referring the Government to the fiscal
advantages the free sale of this article is now producing in
Portugal ; and that probably in no other country the complete suppression of the customs would bring more beneficial
results than in the islands of Cuba and Porto-Rico, which,
besides producing the economical effect of increasing their
commerce and wealth would raise a serious obstacle against
the tendencies towards territorial extension, which on some
future day may again develop itself, as the possession of Cuba,
after the suppression of the customs, would no longer offer
them any mercantile advantage, and as these form the most
important links of the federation, all project for the annexation of Cuba would have to contend against the unpopularity
of re-establishing an odious institution : that while that great
reform is not realized, the monopoly of the flag should be
suppressed, for it has harmed none so much as the Spanish
shipping itself, for whose benefit it was established ; and as
soon as possible such necessary franchises should be created
so that the importation of products on deposit in the island
of Cuba, be at once realized for owing to her geographical
position, she is destined to be in America, the great commercial depot between the old and new worlds, and to possess
thus a fountain of wealth.

III.

The first of the interrogatories investigates the reforms of
which the organization of slave labor is susceptible ; and if
strict measures are convenient for the suppression of vagrancy

among free blacks; if the law which rules Asiatic colonization can be improved, and which kind of immigration best suits Cuba or Porto Rico.

At the outset we notice most prominent among all those questions, the one concerning slavery. Unfortunate institution! which, having always been a moral evil, is to-day a source of most imminent internal and external danger, which now threatens our ultramarine provinces and compromises the dignity and peace of the Spanish nation.

It is necessary before all things and with the sincerity of honest men to do away completely with the African slave-trade, which has been so far the unextinguishable supplier of slaves in the Antilles. I will not delay on the political and moral considerations which advise more energetic and efficient measures than those last ones taken by the government: it is not long since in the Senate I had occasion to discuss them publicly and they are denied by no one; what I will now do is to repeat the effort with which I unavailingly pretended that the commerce of African slaves should be considered piracy, not so much with the object of aggravating the material punishment of the culprits, as with the view of giving to the world a proof that we are in accord with the enlightened nations that anathematized that infamous commerce with a similar declaration. Even if it were not an efficient measure in its repressive action, the fear of loss of nationality more than that of life, would always claim for it the highest considerations of policy. Let us bear in mind that the slave-trade question seriously involves the honor of the Spanish nation, the sincerity of which has been doubted, unfortunately owing to circumstances that have told against us; let it also be remembered that nations as well as individuals should not only be honest but endeavor to appear so; and Spain should prove with *facts* that she sincerely wishes to suppress the slave-trade by following the path of other nations in proscribing and condemning this trafic in human beings.

I clearly see the inefficiency of this declaration, or the registering of slaves, or even the greatest vigilance to do away with this horrible commerce in Africa whilst a market offering rich profits to smugglers and slavery exists.

But if no reason could be found for a prudent, far-seeing and patriotic government to encounter obstacles which the arduous social problem in the Antilles present, this very reason justifies a determination which, being laid before us by all religious and moral precepts, will in a great measure serve to dispel the future political horizon of Spain.

Slavery, that in history has been an universal institution, almost extinct with the last remains of the middle ages, but reappeared after the conquest of America, painful as its confession must be, is only now a Spanish institution, as Brazil, though not having abolished it yet, has promised to occupy herself in the solution of this problem. We well know the great sacrifices made for freeing the four million African slaves in the United States of America, part of whose territory is only six hours distant from Havana.

We also are aware of this gigantic event being accomplished when more than once resolutions were proposed in Congress for prohibiting the importation of all products raised by slave labor; this would completely ruin Cuba, as the United States buy over half her products.

Slavery is a question of humanity, and while we maintain it in our ultramarine provinces will afford a pretext for foreign intervention, and subject us to the disturbances and humiliations incident thereto. As societies for the abolition of slavery are maintained in England, France and Spain, and these societies have a strong hold on the popular sympathies and daily gain ground in public opinion, they will end by creating a moral coalition which will prove irresistible.

That we may be able to act with prudence and freedom in the position made for us by these circumstances, let Spain take the first step : lest by refusing to do so we be caught by the abolition current and swept along at blind speed, compelled to sacrifice all interests, with no reasonable hope of compensation to proprietors. For this, the moment is now propitious and the circumstances favorable.

Had the noble and generous impulses by which the legislatots of 1810 were inspired been effectively carried, Spain would not now be,—and it is a consoling reflection,—the last of Christian nations to abolish slavery ; but a mistaken paternal regard for the American Provinces brought about a reaction. and prevented this result.

At that time the abolition of slavery was desired, but could not be realized by the Cortes owing to the numerous petitions from various bodies of these provinces against the measure.

In quieter times this opposition would but have produced a modification of the proposed measure. This, unfortunately, the troubled state of the country prevented ; and since that time, the slave trade having continued, the number of slaves have increased at such a rate as to largely increase the present difficulties.

That the proprietors of the Antilles are now foremost in recognizing the necessity of carefully studying the situation, is shown by the various representations to the Government authorities ; and that they desire a satisfactory solution of the problem is proven by the numerous pamphlets, proposing various plans for abolition, which are printed and circulated largely among them.

The proposition to now carry out great reforms in the regime of the Antilles creates an opportunity for the Government to offer economical and political compensation: and to decide with the proprietors of slaves the merit and responsibility of abolition.

And as at this moment the most important internal questions engage the attention of the United States, Spain can act with all the freedom necessary to success : and can beside count upon the active co-operation of the proprietors, and may expect the freedman's gratitude for an act of spontaneous justice ; as well as the praise and approval of civilized nations. Not to take advantage of so many favoring circumstances would exhibit a great lack of political foresight.

Now, in my opinion what Government should do,—and do before future events, now visible, press themselves forward to embarass its action,—is, to immediately do away with the twin fountains of slavery,—the commerce and birth of slaves, and by so doing satisfy universal opinion, render a tribute to justice, and lay the foundation for a complete resolution of the problem.

I am not blind to the strong objections which may be urged against free birth ; but it must be borne in mind that great evils call for strong remedies,—that life cannot be preserved in a sick body without some damage ; and that to save a part, a man often submits to the painful amputation of one of his members.

Free birth, with a clause providing that the owners of mothers preserve their character as patrons over the children, with obligation of bringing them up, and a right to their gratuitous services up to 21 years of age, would prevent many evils ; because, while securing to those born after the passage of such a law, proper care and apprenticeship to labor, it gives a return to the patron of the gratuitous services of a useful man for at least six years.

I do not think free birth enough : something more should be done in my opinion, such as taking advantage of the partial liberation system, with which slaves and owners are well acquainted both in Cuba and Porto-Rico, and with the conviction that the tender and solicitous habits in both Antilles, and that the Christian spirit of our slave legislation has stopped the growth of odious and profound enmities, that in other countries have caused great difficulty in the gradual emancipation of slaves.

This gradual emancipation is possible in Cuba, where, may be, there is hardly a slave that has not among his friends or relations a free or partially free man.

I believe also, that through respect due to property acquired under the authority of law, and in order that the co-operation of the proprietors, which ought not to be doubted, may facilitate the successful issue of this great moral and patriotic enterprise, of emancipating the slaves in the Spanish Dominions, it would be prudent and advantageous, as under less favorable circumstances was done by Holland, for the

Government to consult the proprietors, up to a definite period and under the form it may think best, (and certainly none could be better in such a matter than the vote of the Insular and Provincial Deputations, if they should be instituted) before the formation of a definite plan of emancipation, animated by the conviction that the abolition of slavery ought not to be delayed. It is clear that I do not attach much importance to reforming the laws, as indicated in the Interrogatories relative to slaves. Besides, notwithstanding the severity of their laws, they are, as a general rule, sufficient to insure good treatment, it having fallen to my lot to push forward and put in execution, during my command in Cuba, one of these laws, which has done away with many abuses.

As a general rule, I have said, because horrible exceptions cannot be wanting where slavery exists ; and inspired by the painful remembrance that I have of some of them, I must indicate two reforms which I consider proper to apply whilst slavery exists, and above all things, very advantageous as a preliminary for abolition.

The first of these refers to the right which the owners possess of flogging their slaves ; for though the law limits the number of lashes to twenty-five, yet it allows in this limit the possibility of a cruel torture, which endangers life, without its being sufficient to restrain the anger which impels this always barberous style of punishment. I am made aware, through most worthy testimony, that there are in Cuba several sugar estates where flogging has been proscribed, and which have succeeded in maintaining order and discipline among their slaves ; this proves that corporal punishment is unnecessary for preserving the strictest discipline; and if this proof is enough for its being abolished, with more reason should it be done when we bear in mind that it is inflicted always without reflection and calmness of mind, and on many occasions most distinguished persons, and even ladies of the best society have made themselves delinquents whilst in the excitement of an offence.

The abolition of corporal punishment will be a new conquest in the cause of humanity ; a good corrollary to the one

that dispossessed the masters some time ago of the right of
life and death, and will establish that the objection does not
lie against one or more lashes, but against the lash itself, in
the material injury caused our neighbor ; awakening moral
feelings so sadly corrupted by slavery, and thus making
more respectable the slave and less hateful the owner, and
will leave them better prepared for their mutual relations
after this servile institution has been removed.

The second consideration relates to the accessory penalty
now imposed upon masters in cases of cruelty towards slaves,
compelling them to sell or otherwise change the abused slave.

As in the ancient Roman, so in the modern Spanish legislation, a progressive march may be observed, during which
the slave looses by degrees the condition of a thing, and ac-
quires that of a person. Let us, obedient to this march, and
impelled by those principles of justice respected by all the
world, declare that the time has come when the accessory
penalty should be more effectively used for the benefit of the
slave, and afford compensation where the wrong was committed,—ill-treatment of the slave being punished not by his
forced sale, but by his liberation. This change in the direction of right and justice would be a preliminary step toward
emancipation.

Proceeding to the subject of free blacks ; it is evident from
statistics that they are more industrious than the whites in
the island of Cuba ; and I can aver that the cases of vagrancy among that class are very rare, and not sufficient to
justify any measures of compulsion. The project of organizing free labor, repelled by all the civilized world, is particularly rejected in the islands of Cuba and Porto-Rico; in the
first, an attempt was made at establishing rules for the hands
in tobacco factories, on whose evident inconveniences several
corporations of the island have reported extensively and with
reason; and in the latter, regulations are in vogue not sustained in the execution, and against which the enlightened
opinion of the country is to-day clamorous.

If, on the other hand, we take into consideration the want
of labor which is constantly felt in the island of Cuba,—the

supply of which cannot be overlooked, and ought above all things to be attended to with the greatest care in carrying into effect the social changes contemplated,—it will be clear that in order to bring about a supply of labor, which may in some measure correspond to the demand, what we require are franchises and not obstacles.

As regards Asiatic colonization, I can say nothing further than that I disapproved of it publicly and energetically from the moment I was in a position to appreciate the abuses to which it was liable, and which I found to be similar to those of the African slave-trade. Asiatic colonization, such as is carried on to-day, is, notwithstanding the laws, a real temporary slavery, with all the inconveniences of a permanent institution of the kind. In whatever way it may be carried on, it will always be an evil for the island of Cuba, where, for many years, all efforts should tend towards assuring the preponderance of the white race, and where the mixture of a third, inimical to the two already existing, and balanced in numbers, cannot but serve to raise additional clouds in the horizon, which is unfortunately yet very dark in our precious Antille.

The erroneous idea,—and which, notwithstanding its erroneousness, has received great credence,—that the white race cannot withstand agricultural labor in the fields of the tropics, has been disproved upon many plantations in the island of Cuba and especially of Porto-Rico : and from the moment the aptitude of the white race for such labor has been demonstrated, it becomes the duty of all those who take an interest in the prosperity of the Antilles to promote white immigration by all possible means, it being the only one that does not threaten in these provinces future dangers.

I do not believe that the Spanish Peninsula has such an excess of population that she can afford to provide the ultramarine provinces with a numerous and productive immigration of Spaniards, although, undoubtedly, that would be the most acceptable to the Cubans, and although, according to the prevailing doctrine on the subject of immigration, it is considered as a source of material prosperity and of increase

of population for the countries from which emigratio pro
ceeds. But the fact is, that a considerable emigration of
Spaniards from the Peninsula, does really take place, but in
order to avoid the persecution which claims them to recuper-
ate the army in Cuba, they go, rather, to the Spanish-
American Republics, where they but serve to entangle their
country in international conflicts.

To discover the means by which this Spanish emigration
may be directed to Cuba, should be the duty of the Government, for success in that direction would be a guaranty of
peace and safety,—a fountain of prosperity and riches.

But the ports of the Antilles ought not to be closed to
foreign immigration on this account : an immigration, which
under present circumstances can only come from Europe,—
for the inhabitants of the American continent possess an im-
mense territory, equal in richness to that of the Antilles, and
which there exists no reason for their abandoning.

I have never seen the dangers which others dream, in the
possible immigration of strangers to the island of Cuba, but
I do see dangers, and I see further a flagrant injustice in the
special legislation which denies all liberty of political action
to strangers who come to its shores ; and by virtue of the reciprocity upon which depend a nation's rights, subjects the
Spaniards of the Antilles to the same legal disabilities in
fareign countries. The Royal Order of 1817 concerning population, frequently repeated in its restrictive decrees in
proclamations and other legislative acts, and though contrary to the commercial code, which appears to permit the
entrance of transient foreigners, its spirit prevails, and it is a
fact that a stranger cannot remain over three months in
Cuba without being domiciled, and that in order to be
domiciled he has to profess the Catholic religion and take an
oath of allegiance, which is equivalent to renouncing his
nationality. This is not always carried rigorously into effect
because there is something more imperious than the laws in
the spirit of men and the Government : but that is legally
the truth. This is one of the points on which, in my judgment, the natives of the Antilles have a complete right to

deprived of the benefit of the treaties negotiated by the Spanish nation, and that the Royal Decree of the 17th November, 1852, which regulates the treatment of strangers in Spain, be extended to the ultramarine provinces, and which according to the principle of reciprocity to which I have before alluded, is the basis upon which is founded the rights of Spaniards in foreign countries.

In advocating the similarity of institutions with the Peninsula, I urge the expediency of making the political or civil structure of the Government independent of the military command in the grades common to both countries, and I say nothing in reference to the superior civil Government, which in Cuba is a special appointment. I will now add that in my judgment, that high office ought to be confided to a statesman, gifted with the same qualifications that are required in a minister of the crown, and I think that in this respect the conduct of England towards her colonies is worthy of imitation, inasmuch as she elects the man without considering whether he belongs to the military profession or not. If a military man as a matter of course he must belong to the grade of generals, and I see no reason why in such a case he should not hold both the civil government and the Superior command of the army, but if the Superior government be entrusted to a civilian, I see no reason why the army should not be commanded by a general who should be independent of the civil governor, although related to each other by determined laws in regard to reciprocal aid, and who should in case of war or rebellion, assume supreme command.

Such is the report which I find it my duty to make to your Excellency concerning the reforms which should be carried out in the political, economical and social government of the Antilles. I assure your Excellency that in drawing up this report I have completely ignored the fact that I am a party man, and that the party to which I belong is to-day in opposition to the one of whose cabinet your Excellency forms a part. I see in the reform of the regime of the Antilles a question of great national importance, and shall always be disposed to give my hearty praises to that minister, whoever he may be, who will have the glory to accomplish it and thus succeed in securing to Spain the perpetual preservation of her rich and flourishing ultramarine provinces ; so that each day our flag may acquire fresh sympathy and respect in the world discovered. conquered and civilized by the heroism and christian spirit of our forefathers.

FRANCISCO SERRANO.

MADRID, May 10th, 1867.